Business Cybersecurity for Entrepreneurs & Freelancers

How to Secure Customer Data, Email, Payments, and Your Online Business from Cyber Threats

By Joe Correa

Published by Live Stronger Faster

This book is for educational and informational purposes only. The author and publisher are not engaged in rendering legal, financial, or other professional advice. Readers should consult a qualified professional before making any financial decisions.

First Edition

Table of Contents

Introduction

Running your own business is one of the most empowering and liberating decisions you can make. Whether you're a freelance designer, a virtual assistant, a digital marketer, or an e-commerce entrepreneur, you've likely embraced the freedom of working on your own terms. But as the modern business world becomes increasingly digital, this freedom comes with a new and very real risk: cyber threats. For every moment you gain in flexibility and independence, there's a potential vulnerability lurking in the background—from hackers targeting your email to malware infecting your website.

The truth is, entrepreneurs and freelancers are among the most common targets of cyberattacks—not because they're careless, but because they're busy. You wear every hat in your business: marketing, client relations, operations, finances, and more. That often means cybersecurity gets pushed to the bottom of your to-do list, or worse, ignored completely. And yet, a single phishing attack, a stolen password, or an insecure website can shut down your income stream overnight. Cybersecurity isn't just something "tech people" need to worry about—it's a vital business survival skill for anyone making money online.

You might think you're too small to be noticed, but that's exactly what cybercriminals are counting on. While big companies have IT departments and robust security infrastructure, most solo business owners don't have time or money to invest in complex systems. Hackers know this—and they've developed sophisticated yet simple ways to exploit small businesses. It's often easier to steal credit card numbers from an unprotected freelancer's e-commerce store than to break into a Fortune 500 server. The size of your business doesn't determine your risk level—your level of cybersecurity awareness does.

The good news is, you don't need to become a cybersecurity expert to protect your business. You just need to learn some simple, practical strategies and adopt smart habits. That's where this book comes in. We've created a clear, step-by-step guide designed specifically for entrepreneurs, freelancers, solopreneurs, side hustlers, and creators who want to keep their business and client data secure—without overwhelming tech jargon or expensive tools. You'll learn how to secure your email, protect your website, avoid scams, keep client files safe, and make smarter decisions about the tools you use every day.

In this book, we'll start by helping you understand why cyberattacks happen, and what hackers are actually looking for when they target small businesses. We'll then walk you through setting up a basic but strong digital foundation—covering device protection, password managers, and two-factor authentication. From there, you'll learn how to keep your email and communications private, how to prevent common e-commerce threats, and how to protect sensitive client data when you work remotely or collaborate with others. We'll even teach you how to spot red flags, create backup systems, and respond quickly if you ever get hacked.

This book isn't just about avoiding disaster—it's about creating confidence. When you secure your business, you gain peace of mind. You know that your clients' information is safe. You know that a single cyber event won't destroy the work you've built. And more importantly, you can proudly showcase your cybersecurity practices as a professional differentiator. Clients trust providers who treat their information with care. In fact, many businesses are now requiring freelancers and contractors to meet basic security standards before working together. This book will help you meet those expectations—and exceed them.

As a freelancer or business owner, your reputation is everything. A breach of client data, even by accident, can tarnish your brand and cost you thousands of dollars in lost work and damaged trust. But most breaches aren't due to highly sophisticated attacks. They're caused by simple oversights: clicking a bad link, using the same password across multiple sites, or failing to install a security update. By becoming more aware of these weak points and putting easy safeguards in place, you can dramatically reduce your risk.

Every chapter in this book is built for action. We'll give you not just information, but concrete steps and checklists you can follow today. You don't need to pause your business or hire an expert. In most cases, you can start implementing better cybersecurity practices in under 30 minutes. As you go, you'll find recommendations for free or affordable tools that simplify your workflow while keeping you protected.

This is not a technical manual. It's a real-world survival guide for entrepreneurs who want to build a thriving, secure online business. Whether you're just starting out or have been freelancing for years, the time to secure your business is *now*. The digital world is evolving fast—but with the right mindset and methods, you can stay one step ahead.

So if you're ready to stop leaving your business exposed, and start protecting what you've worked so hard to build, let's begin. Cybersecurity isn't just about avoiding threats—it's about building a safer, more resilient foundation for your freedom and success.

Chapter 1: Why Cybersecurity Matters for Entrepreneurs

As an entrepreneur or freelancer, your livelihood often depends on a laptop, a smartphone, and a reliable internet connection. These tools give you flexibility, reach, and scalability—but they also make you a target. Understanding *why* cybersecurity matters is the first step toward building a strong digital defense. This chapter explores the key reasons cybercriminals focus on solo businesses, the consequences of ignoring digital safety, and the foundational mindset you need to protect your work, your income, and your clients.

First, let's break a myth: Cyberattacks aren't just aimed at big companies. In fact, small businesses make up a majority of successful cybercrime targets. Why? Because they're perceived as low-hanging fruit. Large companies invest heavily in security infrastructure. They have entire departments dedicated to monitoring threats, setting up firewalls, and scanning for vulnerabilities. Small business owners, on the other hand, often operate alone or with a small team—and assume they're too small to matter. That's exactly the kind of thinking cybercriminals rely on.

Most solo entrepreneurs don't even realize how much sensitive data they handle daily. Whether you're storing client contracts, collecting emails for a newsletter, processing payments, or using third-party platforms like Stripe, PayPal, Notion, Canva, or Google Drive—you're constantly managing private data. If even one of those platforms is compromised, the ripple effect can damage your business, your client relationships, and your reputation.

Let's look at the real cost of a cyberattack on a small business. It's not just about losing files or a few dollars. A single phishing scam can lock you out of your email. A malware infection could shut down your e-commerce store. A ransomware attack could encrypt all your files, including client deliverables, unless you pay a fee—often in untraceable cryptocurrency. Beyond the technical damage, there's something even harder to fix: lost trust. If your clients discover their data was mishandled or leaked, they may never return, and negative reviews or legal consequences could follow.

This is especially dangerous for freelancers who rely on platforms like Upwork, Fiverr, or direct referrals. Your reputation is your brand. One incident can affect your profile ratings, lead to account suspension, or force you to start over on new platforms. For entrepreneurs running coaching businesses, membership sites, or digital product stores, a hacked website could not only disrupt sales but also jeopardize thousands of users' private data. These are not rare cases—they happen every day, and most victims never thought it would happen to them.

So what exactly are hackers after? It's not always about stealing millions. Often, it's about accumulating data: names, emails, passwords, payment info, and access credentials. Even basic client information—like home addresses, signed agreements, or personal preferences—can be valuable on the dark web. Hackers might sell this data, use it for identity theft, or leverage it to break into larger systems. And they often use automated tools to scan the internet for vulnerable websites, unsecured databases, or outdated software.

Entrepreneurs are also targets for impersonation scams. A hacker might hijack your email or social media account and pretend to be you—sending fake invoices, manipulating clients, or asking for sensitive access. The result? Confused clients, canceled contracts, and potentially irreparable damage to your business relationships. If you're running a brand based on trust, transparency, and personal communication, this kind of breach can be devastating.

That's why cybersecurity is no longer optional—it's a core part of running a business online. Just like you wouldn't run a physical store without locks or security cameras, you shouldn't run an online business without basic digital protection. The good news is that you don't need a cybersecurity degree to be safe. You just need awareness, consistent practices, and a willingness to take security as seriously as you take your craft or product.

In this book, you'll learn how to protect your devices, secure your email and passwords, build trust with clients by safeguarding their information, and create backup plans in case anything goes wrong. But most importantly, you'll develop a new mindset: one where cybersecurity becomes a habit, not a chore. Just like brushing your teeth or checking your bank account, digital protection should become part of your daily business routine.

To summarize this chapter, here are the five main takeaways:

1. **You are a target.** Freelancers and solo entrepreneurs are attractive to hackers because they're easy to exploit.

2. **You handle sensitive data.** Whether you realize it or not, you're responsible for client and business information that must be protected.

3. **The cost of inaction is high.** A single breach can damage your income, reputation, and client trust.

4. **Hackers use automation.** They scan for weaknesses constantly—so assuming you're invisible online is dangerous.

5. **Cybersecurity is a habit.** With the right mindset and systems, you can build strong protection without tech overwhelm.

As we move into the next chapters, we'll break this down step by step, showing you exactly how to secure each part of your business. But remember, it starts here—with the commitment to take digital security seriously. You've worked hard to build your business. Let's make sure it's built on a safe foundation.

Samantha, the freelancer.

When Samantha launched her freelance copywriting business, all she needed was a laptop and Wi-Fi. Clients started finding her through referrals, and soon, she had steady work from startups, online coaches, and marketing agencies. Her setup was lean and efficient—just the way she liked it. She used a basic website, a Gmail account, and PayPal for payments. Cybersecurity? That felt like something big companies worried about. She never gave it a second thought.

Until the morning she couldn't access her email.

She woke up to frantic messages on WhatsApp and Instagram: "Hey, did you mean to send this invoice?" "Why are you asking for crypto payments?" "Are you okay?" Her inbox had been hacked. The attacker had impersonated her, emailed her clients, and sent them a new set of banking details to wire payments to. Two clients had already sent money—straight to the hacker. Another had shared confidential content for a campaign that was now exposed. Samantha was shocked. She hadn't clicked any strange links. She hadn't noticed anything wrong. But somewhere, a password had been compromised, and it only took one breach to unravel everything.

In a matter of hours, her client trust was damaged. One client canceled. Another demanded she pay for the stolen funds. Her Upwork account was flagged for suspicious behavior, and her main Google account—tied to everything from documents to calendar appointments—was now locked for review. She felt like her business was slipping through her fingers.

It took weeks to clean up the mess. She hired a tech expert to help her reset her accounts, create new security layers, and reach out to every client with an explanation and apology. While most were understanding, the experience left a mark on her business—and on her confidence. "I thought I was too small to be targeted," she told herself over and over. "Why would anyone hack *me*?"

Samantha's story isn't unique. All over the world, freelancers and small business owners experience cyberattacks that leave them financially and emotionally drained. And it often starts with the belief that cybersecurity is someone else's problem.

But here's the thing: small businesses are the most vulnerable because they're the least protected. Samantha had never used two-factor authentication. Her passwords were reused across platforms. She didn't back up her client files, and she never thought to use a password manager. None of these things were hard to fix—but they weren't even on her radar until it was too late.

After the incident, Samantha rebuilt her business—this time, with security at its core. She started using encrypted email tools and installed a secure password vault. She created client folders with restricted access and educated herself on phishing scams and common attacks. Not only did her business become safer, but her clients noticed too. One even said, "I really appreciate how serious you are about protecting my data. It's why I keep working with you."

What was once a weakness became a competitive advantage.

Today, Samantha mentors new freelancers. She includes cybersecurity in every conversation. Her motto? "Your business is only as strong as your weakest login." She knows now that cybersecurity isn't something you deal with *after* a crisis—it's what you do *to prevent* one.

Like Samantha, you might feel overwhelmed at first. You might wonder where to start. But as her story shows, small steps can make a big difference. And once you make cybersecurity a part of your business routine, you'll never look at your digital tools the same way again.

Chapter 2: Securing Your Devices and Accounts

Your business starts with you—and that means the first layer of protection must begin with the devices and accounts you use every day. Think of your laptop, smartphone, tablet, and even your smartwatch as digital keys to your entire income stream. If any one of these is compromised, everything from client data to bank account access could be at risk. That's why securing your devices and online accounts is the foundation of business cybersecurity.

Let's begin with your **devices**, starting with your computer. Whether you're using Windows or macOS, make sure your operating system is always up to date. Updates often include critical security patches designed to close holes that hackers exploit. Delaying an update by even a few days can leave your system exposed. Set your system to install updates automatically and reboot regularly. This one habit alone protects you from a large percentage of known threats.

Next, install **antivirus and anti-malware software**—and make sure it's running. Many business owners rely on default protections that come with their operating system, like Windows Defender, but adding a trusted third-party tool like Malwarebytes, Norton, or Bitdefender can greatly enhance your defenses. These tools run quietly in the background, scanning for suspicious activity, blocking malicious files, and alerting you when something's not right.

Encryption is another key protection most people overlook. If your laptop or smartphone is ever lost or stolen, encryption ensures that the data stored on your device is unreadable without a passcode or biometric login. On Macs, this feature is called FileVault. On Windows, it's BitLocker. Enabling full-disk encryption takes just a few clicks but provides powerful protection. Make sure you use a secure login and don't leave your device unlocked in shared or public spaces.

When it comes to **mobile devices**, many freelancers and entrepreneurs rely on their phones to manage email, payment apps, and two-factor authentication. That means your phone is a gateway to everything. Secure it with a complex passcode (not just 4 digits), fingerprint or facial recognition, and remote wipe capabilities in case it gets stolen. Use Apple's "Find My" or Google's "Find My Device" features to track, lock, or erase your phone if it falls into the wrong hands.

Once your hardware is secure, it's time to protect your **accounts**—starting with passwords. The easiest way to get hacked is by using weak, reused passwords across multiple sites. If a hacker obtains one of your passwords (say, from a leaked database), they'll use it to try logging into every other account you have. This is called credential stuffing, and it works shockingly well.

To stop this, use a **password manager** like 1Password, Bitwarden, or LastPass. These tools generate and store long, random, unique passwords for each of your accounts. You only need to remember one master password—the app takes care of the rest. Many also come with browser extensions and mobile apps for convenience. Using a password manager isn't just about security—it makes your life easier. No more forgotten passwords, password resets, or insecure notes in your phone.

In addition to strong passwords, always enable **two-factor authentication (2FA)** wherever possible. This is one of the most effective ways to block unauthorized access—even if someone has your password. With 2FA enabled, logging in requires a second step, like entering a code from an app (e.g., Authy, Google Authenticator) or receiving a push notification. Avoid SMS-based codes when possible, as these can be intercepted via SIM swapping attacks. Authenticator apps are more secure and just as easy to use.

Be mindful of your **login sessions**. Many people forget to log out of important accounts on shared or public devices. If you work at a co-working space or use a friend's computer, make sure you always log out of all platforms. Additionally, check your devices for active sessions regularly and terminate any unknown or outdated ones. Services like Google, Dropbox, and Facebook allow you to view all devices where you're currently signed in.

Don't forget about **browser security**. Your browser holds enormous power: saved logins, credit card details, and browsing history. Use browser extensions like HTTPS Everywhere, Privacy Badger, and uBlock Origin to block trackers and ensure secure connections. Disable auto-fill for sensitive information like credit cards, and clear your cookies and cache regularly. If you want an added layer of privacy, consider using privacy-focused browsers like Brave or Firefox.

Finally, back up your devices. No matter how secure you are, things happen—viruses, hard drive failures, accidental deletions. Use both **cloud backups** (such as iCloud, Google Drive, or Dropbox) and **local backups** (such as external hard drives or Time Machine) to protect your most important files. Make sure your backups are encrypted and tested regularly. Backing up is your insurance policy for everything else you do in cybersecurity.

To recap, here's your security checklist for devices and accounts:

1. **Keep your operating systems updated** (automatic updates on).
2. **Install antivirus and anti-malware software** and run scans regularly.
3. **Enable full-disk encryption** on all computers and phones.
4. **Secure your mobile devices** with biometrics, strong passcodes, and remote wipe features.
5. **Use a password manager** to generate and store strong, unique passwords.
6. **Enable 2FA** on all major accounts and avoid SMS-based codes when possible.
7. **Log out of accounts** on shared/public devices and monitor your session history.
8. **Secure your browser** using extensions and privacy tools.
9. **Back up your data** using both cloud and physical devices, with encryption.

Remember, your devices and accounts are the front doors to your business. Leaving them unprotected is like leaving your home unlocked in a high-crime neighborhood. Taking the time to secure your digital tools now will save you from costly disasters down the line.

Carlos story

Carlos had just finished designing a new client website, a sleek landing page for a product launch set to go live the next morning. He worked late into the night, tweaking color schemes and refining headlines until everything was perfect. Proud and exhausted, he closed his laptop and went to bed. But the next morning, something was off.

He tried logging into his email to send the final link, but his password didn't work. He tried again. Still nothing. Then he noticed something worse: several of his social media accounts were locked out too. In a panic, he grabbed his phone to log in from another app—only to find his Instagram had posted a strange ad for a cryptocurrency scam. His heart sank.

Carlos had been hacked.

It all started with a reused password.

A few weeks earlier, one of the platforms he subscribed to had suffered a data breach. His email and password combination had been leaked onto the dark web, and from there, automated bots began testing those credentials on every popular platform—Google, Facebook, Instagram, PayPal, even his domain registrar. The password worked on five of them. Within hours, the attackers had taken over his digital identity.

Carlos wasn't completely tech-illiterate. He considered himself pretty savvy. He used antivirus software on his laptop and backed up his files to Google Drive. But like many freelancers, he underestimated just how vulnerable he really was. He had the same password for multiple services. He'd never enabled two-factor authentication. His laptop had no encryption. And his phone didn't even have a lock screen password—he thought Face ID was too annoying to set up.

As he started cleaning up the damage, the realization hit hard. The hackers had not only accessed his client files and contracts, but they'd also sent phishing emails pretending to be him. One client wired $1,200 to a fraudulent account. Another was furious that her unpublished project had been compromised. Even his domain was briefly redirected to an adult site. He felt exposed and embarrassed.

That week, Carlos couldn't work. Instead, he was on customer support calls, filing reports, and trying to prove to clients—and to himself—that he was still trustworthy. One client ended their contract. Another said they'd consider coming back in a few months. "We just can't take that risk right now," they said.

It wasn't just a hack—it was a business crisis.

After the dust settled, Carlos made a decision: this would *never* happen again. He began researching cybersecurity for entrepreneurs and quickly realized how easy many of the fixes were—if only he had known about them sooner.

He started with his **passwords**. He signed up for a password manager, deleted all his old reused logins, and created strong, unique ones for every account. He used two-factor authentication for everything—from email to payment apps—and opted for app-based codes instead of SMS, which he now knew could be intercepted.

Next, he secured his **devices**. He enabled full-disk encryption on his laptop and phone. He installed reputable antivirus software, turned on automatic updates, and stopped clicking "remind me later" every time a system patch came out. He even removed old apps he no longer used—some of which hadn't been updated in years and posed security risks.

He looked at his **browser habits** too. He started using a privacy-focused browser and installed extensions to block trackers and malicious scripts. He disabled auto-fill for credit cards and cleared his history regularly. He removed dozens of saved logins that were stored insecurely in his browser. He even changed how he used public Wi-Fi—no more logging into important accounts from cafés without a VPN.

But perhaps the most important change Carlos made was to his **mindset**. He realized that cybersecurity wasn't just a set of tools—it was a way of thinking. He started reviewing his login history weekly, checking for unknown devices, and backing up his most important files to both cloud and encrypted external drives. He treated his digital tools like an extension of his business—not just accessories, but assets that needed protection.

A month later, Carlos landed a new client, a fast-growing tech startup. During the onboarding call, they asked a question that would've once made him nervous: "How do you handle client data security?"

This time, Carlos smiled. "I use encrypted backups, unique passwords with two-factor authentication, and encrypted cloud storage. Your data will be treated with the same level of care I give my own business."

They were impressed.

Carlos didn't just rebuild his systems—he rebuilt his credibility. And from that point forward, cybersecurity became part of his personal brand. He even created a resource checklist to send to new clients who wanted to improve their own protection. What began as a nightmare turned into a competitive advantage.

His story is a reminder that most entrepreneurs aren't taken down by high-tech hackers with deep pockets. They're taken down by small mistakes—reused passwords, ignored updates, missing 2FA. But every mistake is a chance to learn. And every day is a chance to do better.

Carlos learned that the tools to protect your digital business are available to everyone. You don't need to be a tech expert. You just need to treat your business like it matters enough to protect. Because it does.

And so do you.

Chapter 3: Protecting Client Data and Sensitive Information

As a freelancer or entrepreneur, you are the guardian of the information your clients trust you with. Whether you're a designer handling brand assets, a coach collecting personal goals, or a consultant managing financial records, your business interacts with sensitive data every day. Many professionals underestimate just how much valuable information they collect and store. But protecting client data is not just about ethics or good service—it's a business-critical responsibility that, when ignored, can result in legal trouble, lost income, or permanent reputational damage.

Let's begin with understanding **what qualifies as sensitive data**. This includes names, phone numbers, home addresses, passwords, payment details, signed contracts, personal project files, client notes, brand strategy documents, and even casual DMs or emails that reveal private business intentions. Anything that a client would not want shared or stolen falls into this category. If you collect it, store it, or transmit it—digitally or physically—you are responsible for protecting it.

The first rule of protecting client data is **minimization**. The less data you collect and store, the less there is to lose if something goes wrong. Only gather what you absolutely need.

For example, if you don't need your client's birthday or home address to deliver your service, don't ask for it. If you're done with a project, archive the essential documents and securely delete the rest. Reducing the volume of stored data reduces your risk surface dramatically.

Once you've identified the data you *must* keep, it's time to implement secure **storage practices**. This starts with choosing the right cloud platforms. Services like Google Workspace, Dropbox Business, OneDrive, or iDrive can be secure *if* used properly. Always use the business-grade version of these platforms when possible, and make sure you activate all built-in security settings: password-protected file sharing, 2FA, device access control, and encryption.

File permissions matter too. Avoid sharing documents or folders with "Anyone with the link" settings. Instead, grant access only to specific email addresses—and remove access as soon as it's no longer needed. Regularly audit who has access to what. This is especially important when working with teams or subcontractors. A forgotten shared link or a loose access policy can quickly turn into a major vulnerability.

If you store client files locally (on your computer or hard drive), make sure the **files are encrypted and backed up**. Use tools like VeraCrypt or enable full-disk encryption in your operating system. Keep your external drives secure and hidden—not lying on your desk or in a shared workspace. Never store sensitive data on unsecured USB drives, and avoid transferring client files through unsecured Bluetooth or public Wi-Fi connections.

When sending client documents or gathering personal information, avoid **email attachments** when possible. Instead, use secure file sharing services like Google Drive (with permissions), WeTransfer Pro, or encrypted messaging platforms like ProtonMail or Signal. If email must be used, always double-check recipient addresses and never include passwords or personal identifiers in the body of the message.

Protecting client data also includes using **secure intake forms** and **contract tools**. Platforms like JotForm, Paperform, or Typeform offer HIPAA-compliant options, SSL encryption, and password-protected submissions. If you collect e-signatures or contracts, services like DocuSign, PandaDoc, or HelloSign offer encrypted storage and audit trails. Always look for platforms that explicitly state their data protection standards and certifications.

Another overlooked area is **device access**. If you allow others to use your work computer or tablet—even just for a minute—you open a window to your client data. Make sure all your work devices are locked with biometric or strong password protections, and never leave them unattended in public spaces. If you're collaborating with contractors or team members, ensure they follow minimum security standards and never download client files to unsecured personal devices.

Don't forget about **naming conventions**. Avoid using client names or private details in filenames—especially for shared or publicly accessible links. Instead of "SmithFinancial_PaymentStrategy2025.pdf", use something more neutral like "Client01_InvoicePlan_Q1.pdf". It's a simple habit that minimizes exposure even if file names are accidentally revealed.

Finally, create a clear **data retention and deletion policy**. Know how long you'll keep client data and how you'll destroy it when it's no longer needed. Shred physical documents if you ever print them. Use secure deletion tools like Eraser (Windows) or FileShredder (Mac) to remove digital files completely. Never leave a digital paper trail of old, unused files sitting in your drive for years.

Here's your quick checklist for protecting client data:

1. **Minimize what you collect.** Only store what is essential to the project.

2. **Use encrypted cloud storage.** Opt for business-grade tools with full access controls.
3. **Limit file permissions.** Share only with specific people, and revoke access after project completion.
4. **Encrypt local files.** Enable full-disk encryption and secure your external drives.
5. **Avoid email attachments.** Use secure sharing services with link expiration options.
6. **Choose secure intake and contract platforms.** Look for encryption and compliance standards.
7. **Protect your devices.** Use strong login protections and avoid device sharing.
8. **Be smart with file names.** Keep client identities private in file labeling.
9. **Back up sensitive data securely.** Use encrypted backups and test restoration regularly.
10. **Delete what you no longer need.** Have a clear, scheduled data cleanup routine.

Protecting client data is not just about reducing risk—it's about earning and keeping trust. Clients may never know how secure your systems are, but they'll always feel the difference when you treat their privacy with the same respect you'd want for your own. In a world where data breaches are common, being the professional who takes security seriously is a business edge that sets you apart.

Lena's freelancer story

Lena was a high-performing freelance brand strategist known for her ability to take raw business ideas and turn them into polished visual identities. Over the years, she had worked with dozens of clients—from boutique skincare brands to tech startups—building a solid reputation through word of mouth. Her onboarding process was seamless. Clients would complete a short questionnaire, sign a digital contract, and upload their company documents—financial summaries, business goals, investor pitch decks—everything she needed to craft their brand story.

She didn't think twice about storing it all on her laptop.

One Friday afternoon, Lena got a panicked email from a past client, Alex, who had just pitched to a group of investors using a proprietary presentation. The problem? That same deck had mysteriously appeared on a competitor's website—almost word for word. "You were the only person outside our company who had access to that file," he said. "Did you share it with anyone?"

Lena's heart dropped.

She knew she hadn't shared it intentionally, but the accusation stuck. She scrambled to check her folders. The file was still there, in the same place she'd saved it months ago. She scanned her email and cloud drive—no obvious leaks. Then she checked her Google Drive sharing settings. To her shock, she discovered that one of her shared folders was still marked "Anyone with the link can view." She had used the setting months ago for a temporary collaboration—and forgotten to turn it off.

Worse yet, she found that the link had been indexed by a public search engine. The investor pitch deck—along with two other sensitive files from different clients—had been exposed for weeks. Anyone could have downloaded them. There was no telling who had accessed the folder, or how widely the documents had been shared.

The fallout was swift. Alex pulled the plug on all future collaboration and demanded that Lena cover legal costs for what he called "gross negligence." Another client, whose brand strategy doc was also exposed, emailed her a formal warning and threatened to post a negative review. Lena felt sick. It wasn't just about one mistake—it was about the trust that had quietly eroded without her even knowing it.

For years, Lena had prided herself on professionalism. Her clients saw her as meticulous, organized, and dependable. But the truth was, when it came to data security, she had been careless. She had no formal system for managing sensitive documents. She used personal cloud accounts instead of business-grade tools. She never encrypted her laptop or used password-protected links. And she never, not once, reviewed access permissions after a project was complete.

The damage wasn't just reputational. She lost two active clients, and three more canceled upcoming consultations. The financial hit was brutal—but the emotional toll was worse. For weeks, Lena felt like she had failed at something fundamental.

Eventually, she decided to rebuild—not just her business, but her systems. She invested in business-grade tools for contracts, file sharing, and storage. She upgraded to encrypted cloud platforms with audit trails. She installed a password manager and enabled 2FA on all devices and accounts. She deleted dozens of old project folders she no longer needed, and created a structured retention and deletion policy. Every new client now received a digital confidentiality statement outlining exactly how their data would be handled, stored, and deleted.

Lena also started labeling files differently. No more names or brand specifics in file titles. Instead of "RileyCo_Rebrand_Strategy_Jan2025.pdf," she now used neutral formats like "Client21_Phase1_Strategy.pdf." It was a small detail, but one that added another layer of privacy.

Within months, Lena felt more in control than she had in years. She created a custom onboarding process that included secure forms, encrypted messaging, and automatic access expiration. Clients started commenting on how "professional and secure" her process felt. One even said, "You're the only freelancer I've ever worked with who takes our data this seriously. That's why I refer people to you."

What had once been her biggest vulnerability had become her strongest advantage.

Lena's story is a lesson in both caution and redemption. Data protection isn't always about massive breaches or malicious hackers. Sometimes it's about tiny oversights—a link that wasn't revoked, a document that wasn't renamed, a file that stayed online too long. But even one small lapse can have major consequences.

Today, Lena teaches other creatives how to implement basic cybersecurity into their freelance workflows. She reminds them that protecting client data is more than a technical task—it's a relationship builder. "Trust is fragile," she says. "And privacy is how you protect it."

If you run a client-facing business, Lena's experience is a powerful reminder: privacy isn't a feature—it's a promise. One that's worth keeping, every time.

Chapter 4: Business Email and Phishing Protection

Email is the central nervous system of your business. It's where you communicate with clients, receive invoices, send contracts, reset passwords, and confirm payments. And because of that, it's also one of the most frequent and dangerous targets for cybercriminals. If a hacker gains access to your business email, they can impersonate you, hijack accounts, steal sensitive information, and wreak havoc in ways that are hard to trace and even harder to fix.

For freelancers and entrepreneurs, email security is non-negotiable. It's not just about keeping your inbox clean—it's about protecting your entire business identity.

Let's start with the most common and deceptive threat: **phishing**. These are fake emails that appear to be from trusted sources—like your bank, Google, PayPal, or even a client. They're designed to trick you into clicking malicious links, downloading dangerous files, or entering your login information on fake websites. Phishing emails often create a sense of urgency: "Your account has been suspended," "A payment has failed," or "Click here to confirm your login." They prey on panic—and they work.

To protect yourself, always examine the **sender address** carefully. Phishing emails often use slight misspellings or lookalike domains (like "gma1l.com" instead of "gmail.com"). If something feels off, it probably is. Never click on links or download attachments from unexpected or suspicious emails. When in doubt, go directly to the website in your browser rather than using the link in the email.

You should also **train your eye** to spot common red flags. Poor grammar, generic greetings ("Dear user"), strange formatting, or threats of immediate consequences are all signs of phishing. If you receive a strange email from someone you know—especially if it includes a vague attachment or link—contact them through another channel to confirm it's real.

Now let's talk about **securing your actual email account**. If you're using a free Gmail, Outlook, or Yahoo account for business, consider upgrading to a business-grade email provider like **Google Workspace**, **ProtonMail**, or **Zoho Mail**. These services offer added security features, better spam filtering, and compliance options.

Regardless of your provider, enable **two-factor authentication (2FA)**. This adds a second layer of protection by requiring a temporary code from your phone (via an authenticator app) when logging in. Even if your password is stolen, your account remains safe as long as the attacker doesn't have your 2FA device. Avoid using SMS for 2FA whenever possible, as phone numbers can be hijacked through SIM-swapping attacks. Use an app-based option instead, like Google Authenticator, Authy, or Microsoft Authenticator.

Password hygiene for email is critical. Never reuse your email password for any other service—your email is the master key to everything. If someone breaks into your inbox, they can trigger password resets on dozens of other accounts. Use a long, unique password generated by a password manager, and never share it. If you've been using the same password for years or across platforms, change it immediately.

You should also regularly **audit your inbox and connected apps**. Go into your email settings and check what third-party apps have access to your account. Many people grant permissions to services like social media schedulers, CRM tools, or even random apps they forgot about. Revoke any that you no longer use. These integrations can be entry points for attackers if they're not maintained or properly secured.

Avoid using your personal email account for business activities. Keeping your business and personal communications separate is smart for both security and professionalism. It allows you to limit exposure, compartmentalize your data, and detect suspicious activity faster.

Encrypting your email is another smart layer of protection. While standard Gmail and Outlook do offer some encryption during transmission, tools like **ProtonMail**, **Tutanota**, or **Mailvelope** offer true end-to-end encryption, especially useful when sending or receiving highly sensitive information. You can also use **password-protected attachments** or secure file links when sharing important documents.

When sending email campaigns or automations using tools like Mailchimp or ConvertKit, always use **verified sender domains** and SPF/DKIM records to prevent spoofing. These security protocols ensure that only authorized services can send email on your behalf. Without them, a hacker could spoof your domain and send phishing emails that *appear* to be from you.

Finally, set up **email backups** and monitoring. You can use tools that archive your email to the cloud or a local drive, allowing you to recover messages in case of accidental deletion or breach. Some services also allow alerts for unusual login activity, changes to security settings, or new device logins.

Here's a recap checklist for business email and phishing protection:

1. **Learn to identify phishing emails.** Don't click on links or attachments from unknown or suspicious senders.

2. **Use a business-grade email provider.** Upgrade from free accounts for better protection and compliance.

3. **Enable 2FA with an authenticator app.** Avoid SMS-based codes when possible.

4. **Use a strong, unique password.** Don't reuse your email password anywhere else.

5. **Audit connected apps.** Revoke access to old or unnecessary integrations.

6. **Separate business and personal accounts.** Never mix sensitive information between them.

7. **Use encrypted email or password-protected links.** Avoid sending sensitive data in plain text.

8. **Set up SPF, DKIM, and verified sender settings.** Prevent domain spoofing in email campaigns.

9. **Monitor for suspicious logins.** Set alerts for new device logins and changes to account security.

10. **Back up your emails regularly.** Archive conversations and documents for peace of mind.

Email is both your greatest communication tool and your biggest digital vulnerability. By locking it down with these practices, you're not just avoiding cyberattacks—you're ensuring that your communication, your identity, and your client relationships remain safe and trustworthy.

Now, lets go over Maya's suspicious activity story

Maya was having a great week. She'd just onboarded two new coaching clients and was in talks with a wellness company about a six-month content strategy project. Her calendar was booked, invoices were sent, and things were finally falling into place. On Wednesday morning, while sipping her coffee, she checked her inbox and saw an urgent email from her business bank: "Suspicious Activity Detected on Your Account—Please Confirm Login." Her stomach turned. She clicked the link without hesitation.

What she didn't know was that the email wasn't from her bank. It was a phishing email—designed to look official but crafted by a scammer. The logo, the language, the tone—it all seemed legitimate. The login page even looked identical to her bank's real website. She entered her credentials, submitted the form, and went about her day.

Three hours later, her actual bank called.

"Ms. Rivera, we've noticed several wire transfer attempts from your account totaling over $9,000. Were you expecting to make these transactions today?"

Her heart dropped.

In a panic, Maya opened her email and realized what had happened. The phishing email had tricked her into giving away her login details. She immediately called the bank and froze all outgoing transfers. Some funds were recoverable, but not all. In total, she lost over $2,500—money that had already been withdrawn and routed through accounts that would never be traced. Worse yet, the scammer had access to more than just her bank login. He had access to her email.

That meant the attacker could now view her client conversations, signed contracts, invoices, cloud storage links, and social media reset emails. Within hours, he had sent emails to her clients requesting updated payment details—posing as Maya, asking them to send their deposits to a new account. Two clients responded. One actually sent the money.

Maya's business had been hijacked.

The next few days were a whirlwind of damage control. She reset passwords, sent urgent emails warning clients, contacted platforms like PayPal and Stripe to lock down her accounts, and cried more than once in total disbelief. The clients were kind, but shaken. One paused their coaching package. Another said they'd "circle back in a few months." Maya felt violated, ashamed, and completely overwhelmed. How could this happen so easily?

She'd never thought about securing her email. It was just something she used—like a phone or a notepad. She never enabled two-factor authentication. She reused the same password across multiple accounts. She didn't even realize she'd connected third-party apps to her inbox years ago—tools she no longer used, but which still had permissions to read her email.

It was a painful but transformative wake-up call.

Over the following month, Maya rebuilt her systems from the ground up. She ditched her old Gmail account and created a new one using a business-grade email provider with encrypted storage. She activated two-factor authentication on every account and installed an authenticator app. She downloaded a password manager and created long, random passwords for all her logins. She disconnected all third-party integrations from her email and reviewed her security settings weekly.

She also started learning how to spot phishing emails. She paid attention to sender addresses, spelling errors, and links that didn't match their labels. She began treating every email like a potential trap—not out of paranoia, but caution. She taught herself and her clients how to recognize red flags and how to confirm suspicious messages using separate channels.

Later that year, Maya created a short email security checklist for her newsletter subscribers. It became one of her most opened emails. Clients thanked her for sharing it. Some even said they'd forwarded it to their entire teams. It became clear that Maya wasn't alone—most solo entrepreneurs had no real training in email safety. She was just one of the unlucky ones who had learned the hard way.

Today, Maya shares her story not as a warning, but as a lesson. She reminds her clients that your email is the gatekeeper to your digital life. If someone gets in, they don't just see your messages—they see your identity, your business, your money, your future.

She now begins every client onboarding with a privacy and security statement. It's part of her brand. She doesn't shy away from it—she leads with it. Her clients feel safer, and Maya feels stronger. What once was her biggest vulnerability is now her strongest defense.

Because the truth is, Maya wasn't careless. She was simply unprepared. And now? She's bulletproof.

Chapter 5: Website and E-Commerce Security Basics

Your website is often the first impression your business makes—and for many entrepreneurs and freelancers, it's also the primary way clients find you, learn about your services, and make purchases. But with that visibility comes risk. Your website and e-commerce platforms are public-facing digital assets that cybercriminals routinely scan for vulnerabilities. If left unprotected, they can be hijacked, infected with malware, or used to steal customer data.

Whether you're using WordPress, Wix, Shopify, Squarespace, or a custom-coded site, it's essential to understand how to secure your digital storefront or portfolio from the ground up. In this chapter, we'll cover basic protections that any business owner can implement—no technical background required.

Let's begin with **secure hosting**. Your website is only as secure as the server it's hosted on. Always choose a reputable hosting provider that prioritizes security, offers 24/7 support, daily backups, and SSL certificates. If you're using managed hosting (like Shopify or Squarespace), many of these features are built in. But for platforms like WordPress, you'll need to ensure your hosting company provides malware scanning, DDoS protection, and server-side firewalls.

Speaking of SSL—this is non-negotiable. An **SSL certificate** (Secure Sockets Layer) encrypts the connection between your visitors and your website, keeping sensitive information like passwords and payment data private. When SSL is enabled, your site address starts with "https://" and shows a padlock icon in the browser bar. Not only is SSL essential for security, it also improves your Google rankings and builds customer trust. Most reputable hosting providers offer free SSL certificates—activate it as soon as your site goes live.

Next, let's talk about **platform updates**. If you're using WordPress, Joomla, Magento, or similar platforms, keeping your system up to date is critical. Hackers often exploit known vulnerabilities in outdated themes, plugins, and core files. Set up automatic updates or check for new versions weekly. Delete any unused themes or plugins, as these often go unmonitored and become backdoors for attackers.

Use **strong admin credentials** for your website dashboard and backend tools. This means long, unique passwords stored in a password manager and two-factor authentication enabled wherever possible. Many website hacks happen not because of sophisticated code injection—but because of weak logins like "admin" and "123456." Don't make it easy.

Now, let's focus on **e-commerce security**. If you collect

payments through your site—whether for products, digital downloads, or client services—you must protect both your payment system and your customer data. The easiest way to stay secure is by using a trusted payment gateway like **Stripe, PayPal, or Square**, which handle PCI compliance and encryption on your behalf. Never store credit card information on your own servers. Redirect customers to secure checkout pages hosted by the gateway.

Additionally, enable **CAPTCHA** and **anti-bot protection** on all forms, especially login, signup, and checkout pages. These tools block automated scripts from spamming your system or attempting brute-force login attacks. They may seem like a small annoyance to users, but they're a critical barrier against fraud and abuse.

Install a **security plugin or firewall** if you're on WordPress. Plugins like Wordfence or Sucuri offer malware scanning, IP blocking, brute-force protection, and live traffic monitoring. They alert you if suspicious behavior is detected—like repeated failed login attempts or someone trying to access hidden files.

One of the most important habits to build is **regular backups**. Set your system to automatically back up your site at least once per day, and store a copy both on your hosting server and in an external cloud location like Dropbox or

Google Drive. A hack or server crash shouldn't mean starting over. With a clean backup, you can restore your site in minutes.

Be cautious with **third-party integrations** and plugins. Every tool you add to your website introduces a new potential vulnerability. Only install plugins from trusted sources, check the reviews and update history, and delete any you no longer use. Avoid "nulled" (pirated) themes or plugins—they often contain hidden malware.

Finally, create a habit of **monitoring your website's health**. Use services like Google Search Console, Jetpack, or UptimeRobot to receive alerts if your site goes down or gets flagged for suspicious content. Scan your site for malware weekly, and check your site's loading speed—sudden slowdowns can be a sign of malicious scripts running in the background.

Here's a quick checklist to secure your website and e-commerce platform:

1. **Choose a secure hosting provider.** Look for malware scanning, backups, and firewalls.
2. **Activate SSL encryption.** Ensure your site uses HTTPS with a padlock symbol.

3. **Keep all software updated.** Update plugins, themes, and platforms regularly.

4. **Use strong admin credentials.** Avoid common usernames and always enable 2FA.

5. **Use trusted payment gateways.** Don't store credit card info—let Stripe or PayPal handle it.

6. **Install CAPTCHA on all forms.** Block spam and brute-force attacks automatically.

7. **Add a website firewall/security plugin.** Monitor traffic and prevent malicious access.

8. **Back up your site daily.** Store backups both on-site and off-site.

9. **Limit third-party plugins.** Remove unused tools and verify plugin credibility.

10. **Monitor uptime and security health.** Use alert services to stay informed 24/7.

Your website is your digital storefront—and just like a physical store, it deserves locks, alarms, and insurance. Securing it not only protects your income and your brand but also builds credibility with clients and customers. A secure site says: "I take this business seriously. You can trust me."

How Elijah was hacked

When Elijah launched his online store selling digital planners, he never imagined the back end of his business would one day become his biggest liability. He wasn't a developer, but he had built a clean and simple Shopify store using a drag-and-drop theme, added a few apps for checkout enhancements, and uploaded his products. Sales were steady, his email list was growing, and customers were leaving glowing reviews.

Then one morning, he received a message from a customer that made his stomach drop.

"Hey, I just tried buying your planner but my card got flagged. It said the site might be unsafe. Is everything okay?"

Elijah immediately checked his website. Everything looked normal. The homepage loaded, the products displayed fine, and nothing seemed out of place. But when he tried to check out, a red warning banner popped up: *"This site may be compromised. Proceed with caution."* He clicked into his store admin dashboard—only to find that several apps he hadn't installed were now active, including one called "Fast Checkout Pro++" with code that redirected users to a third-party domain.

He'd been hacked.

A malicious script had been injected through an outdated third-party app. It silently rerouted some users to a spoofed version of his checkout page, where their payment details were harvested without their knowledge. Elijah had no idea how long it had been happening. He hadn't updated his apps in weeks and didn't realize that his hosting didn't automatically perform security scans. The breach cost him more than lost sales—it cost him trust.

Emails started pouring in. One customer reported a fraudulent charge just hours after trying to buy his digital bundle. Another said their bank had frozen their card. Elijah immediately shut down his store and contacted Shopify support, who helped him clean out the corrupted files and remove the rogue scripts. Fortunately, his store was on a managed platform, which made restoring a clean version possible. But the damage had already been done.

Over the next few days, he sent apology emails, offered refunds, and set up a FAQ page explaining what had happened. Most customers were sympathetic. A few weren't. One left a harsh public review: *"Loved the product, but not worth getting hacked over."* His five-star average rating took a hit. So did his confidence.

Elijah took a step back and asked himself what he had missed.

It turned out the list was long: he hadn't enabled two-factor authentication on his admin dashboard, hadn't set up alerts for changes to his website code, and hadn't been backing up his site regularly. Worst of all, he had dozens of inactive apps installed—each a potential open door for hackers.

He decided to rebuild, this time with security as a core principle, not an afterthought. He started by choosing a more secure **e-commerce hosting plan** with daily backups and server-level malware scanning. He activated an **SSL certificate**, even though Shopify offered it by default, and began checking that his links always displayed the padlock icon. He changed all admin login credentials and added a security plugin that monitored code changes and flagged suspicious activity.

He also created a **maintenance checklist**: every Friday, he'd log in, check for updates, run a scan, and manually review form submissions for odd behavior. He limited access to his dashboard and disabled customer account creation unless necessary. He removed every unused plugin and vowed to vet every new one by reading reviews, update history, and developer credentials. No more shortcuts.

To protect checkout flows, he switched to using only **trusted payment gateways**—Stripe and PayPal—and stopped experimenting with third-party checkout add-ons. He updated his privacy policy, added a "Security" section to his website footer, and created a plain-English explanation of how customer data was handled and protected.

Soon, something surprising happened. His customers noticed.

"I appreciate how transparent you've been about data protection," one wrote. "It's part of why I trust buying from you." Another said, "Love that your site feels professional and secure. Some others look sketchy by comparison." In time, his sales rebounded, and his five-star rating started to climb back up.

Elijah learned the hard way that a sleek design and functional store aren't enough. What's behind the curtain matters—and customers can sense it. A secure website isn't just about preventing bad things from happening. It's about signaling that you run a real, responsible business. That their data matters to you. That their trust is earned and protected.

Today, Elijah mentors other solopreneurs launching their first online products. His number one piece of advice? "Don't wait until after a breach to think about website security. Bake it in from day one."

His experience stands as a powerful reminder that your

website is your business's front door. Keep it locked, monitored, and protected—and your customers will feel it, even if they never see it.

Chapter 6: Working with Clients & Remote Teams Securely

As your business grows, collaboration becomes essential. Whether you're sharing files with a client, onboarding a virtual assistant, or outsourcing tasks to a remote contractor, every new interaction introduces a new point of vulnerability. Working with others—especially over the internet—requires not just clear communication, but secure systems that prevent accidental leaks, unauthorized access, and data breaches.

Let's begin with the **principle of least privilege**. This means giving people access only to the information and tools they need to complete their job—nothing more. If you're working with a designer, they don't need access to your entire Google Drive. If you're hiring a social media manager, they don't need full admin access to your payment dashboard. Assign roles carefully. Most cloud platforms—like Google Workspace, Trello, Canva, or Dropbox—allow you to set view-only, comment-only, or editor permissions. Use them.

You should also avoid sharing **raw passwords** through insecure channels like email or text. Instead, use **password managers with sharing capabilities**—such as 1Password Teams or LastPass for Business. These tools let you share access to accounts without ever revealing the actual password.

If you revoke access later, the team member can no longer log in, even if they try.

When using **collaboration tools**, opt for platforms that prioritize encryption and permission controls. Google Drive, Notion, Airtable, and ClickUp all offer access logs, sharing restrictions, and the ability to audit who viewed or edited files. Avoid tools that don't allow you to see who accessed a document or don't notify you of login activity. Transparency and traceability matter when working with others.

Whenever you **onboard a contractor or freelancer**, create a standard procedure for secure access. This might include:

- Creating a temporary email address or alias.
- Sharing only project-specific folders.
- Using time-limited sharing links.
- Sending access instructions via a secure messaging app like Signal or ProtonMail.

Equally important is having a clear **offboarding process**. When someone's contract ends or a project is complete, immediately revoke their access to documents, apps, passwords, and communication channels. Many breaches occur not during a working relationship—but after it ends, when forgotten access points are left open.

Project management tools like Asana, Basecamp, or Monday.com also deserve scrutiny. Ensure users are invited only to relevant projects and that sensitive notes, files, or discussions are kept in private channels if needed. If you're working with sensitive client data—especially in coaching, finance, or health services—always double-check the privacy settings of shared boards and conversations.

If your team works across time zones or countries, be aware of **data privacy regulations**. For instance, if you're collecting client data from the EU, your team must comply with GDPR. That means clear consent, secure storage, and understanding where the data physically resides (some countries restrict data storage outside their borders). Even if you're not legally required to comply, following these guidelines is a smart way to build trust and avoid trouble down the line.

Video calls and recordings are another often overlooked area. If you're recording Zoom calls for training, documentation, or note-taking, make sure all participants are aware, and that the files are stored securely. Avoid keeping recordings on local devices without encryption. Instead, store them in protected folders on cloud services with permission controls.

Emailing files back and forth is one of the least secure ways to collaborate. Use cloud sharing instead. If you *must* send a file via email, encrypt it and send the password separately—preferably via a different communication channel. Even better, upload the file to a secure drive and send a link with view-only access that expires after a set time.

Don't forget about **team training.** If you work with the same contractors or collaborators regularly, invest a little time in teaching them your cybersecurity standards. Send them a simple guide or checklist: use strong passwords, enable 2FA, avoid public Wi-Fi, don't click unknown links, and log out of accounts on shared devices. It might feel unnecessary—but even one weak link can jeopardize your entire operation.

Here's a recap checklist for working securely with clients and remote teams:

1. **Use the principle of least privilege.** Share only what is needed for the job.

2. **Avoid sending passwords directly.** Use password managers with secure sharing features.

3. **Choose encrypted collaboration platforms.** Prioritize tools with access logs and role-based permissions.

4. **Create onboarding procedures.** Share instructions and files using secure, temporary access points.

5. **Have a clear offboarding checklist.** Revoke access immediately after work ends.

6. **Secure project management tools.** Limit who sees what, especially when managing multiple clients.

7. **Know your privacy laws.** Understand GDPR and other data handling requirements if working internationally.

8. **Secure video call recordings.** Inform participants and store recordings in protected folders.

9. **Use cloud links instead of attachments.** Share view-only or time-limited access links.

10. **Educate your team.** Provide security checklists and reinforce safe practices.

In today's digital work environment, collaboration without protection is like leaving your office doors unlocked overnight. Building secure workflows with your clients and collaborators is more than a best practice—it's a professional necessity. It not only protects your data and systems, but it also builds long-term trust and reliability.

I want to talk about Amara's story now.

Amara had built a thriving online business from her home in Atlanta. She offered virtual assistant services to busy executives and entrepreneurs, managing everything from inboxes to travel bookings to calendar coordination. As demand grew, she began assembling a small team of subcontractors—specialists in social media, admin support, and customer service—to help her handle the workload. It felt like her business was finally scaling. But what she didn't realize was that as her team grew, so did her risk.

One Monday morning, a client called her in a panic. "Hey, Amara—I just got an email from someone on your team asking for access to my PayPal. Did you authorize that?" Amara was confused. She hadn't. She pulled up her sent messages. Nothing. She contacted the subcontractor the client mentioned—someone she'd hired just two weeks earlier to help manage invoicing and receipts. The contractor claimed they hadn't sent anything unusual.

But after digging deeper, Amara realized she'd made a critical mistake. During onboarding, she had emailed the new assistant a document with client logins, passwords, and private notes—everything stored in a single, unencrypted Google Doc. She hadn't used a password manager. She hadn't set file access limits. And she hadn't revoked access for a previous assistant whose contract ended a month ago. That document was still accessible—and likely had been copied, shared, or even sold without her knowing.

Worse still, her Google Drive settings were wide open. Dozens of client files had "Anyone with the link can view" permissions. These weren't just calendar templates or brand kits. They included billing statements, contracts, onboarding forms, and private business documents. It was the kind of exposure that could destroy client trust overnight.

Amara felt sick. She called each client personally to explain the situation, apologize, and assure them that she was taking immediate steps to secure their data. Some were understanding. A few were upset. One canceled their contract and asked for a refund. Amara knew she had made a mistake—she had focused on growing her business, but had neglected to protect it.

That night, she couldn't sleep. She realized she'd never thought of herself as someone who "needed" cybersecurity practices. She wasn't a tech company. She didn't handle credit cards. She wasn't storing state secrets. But she was handling *trust*. That was just as valuable—and just as vulnerable.

The next morning, Amara started over. She signed up for a business password manager and moved every login, note, and credential into a secure vault. She changed every shared password and created individual logins for each subcontractor with role-based permissions. No one would ever get full access again—not even temporarily.

She also implemented a formal **onboarding and offboarding** process. Every time she brought someone on, she gave them a specific list of tools they would access—nothing more. She used time-limited file links and never sent credentials over email again. When someone left, she revoked every login immediately. No more forgotten folders or lingering permissions.

She adopted secure platforms for everything: encrypted messaging for sensitive communications, shared drives with permission logs, and project management tools with clear visibility controls. She even recorded a short video walkthrough of her cybersecurity expectations and required every contractor to watch it before accessing any systems.

What had once felt like a chaotic team scattered across time zones now became a well-oiled, secure machine. Files were labeled, organized, and monitored. Every action had a trail. Amara felt in control—not just of the business *output*, but of the *infrastructure* behind it.

Her clients noticed the change too. One emailed, "I just want to say how impressed I am with your professionalism. I've worked with a lot of VAs, and you're the first to have a clear, secure process." Another said, "Thanks for treating my information like it matters."

Amara's mishap didn't end her business—it transformed it. It forced her to level up and create systems that made her brand stronger, not weaker. What began as a breach became a blueprint.

Today, Amara coaches other virtual professionals and service providers on client management. She teaches them that scaling a team isn't just about delegation—it's about security. "If you don't know exactly who has access to what," she says, "then neither do your clients. And that's where trust breaks down."

Her story is a reminder that in the modern business world, collaboration without cybersecurity is a gamble. But with the right systems, you can protect your data, your team, and your reputation—all while growing with confidence.

Chapter 7: Cyber Hygiene and Daily Practices

Cybersecurity isn't a one-time setup—it's a daily practice. Just like brushing your teeth, managing your finances, or checking your calendar, maintaining your digital safety requires consistency, awareness, and small daily habits. This chapter will help you create a personal cybersecurity routine that keeps your devices, accounts, and online business running safely—without overwhelming your schedule or energy.

Let's begin by understanding **what "cyber hygiene" means**. It refers to the regular activities and best practices that keep your digital environment clean, secure, and functioning optimally. Think of it as preventive maintenance for your digital life. Just as you wouldn't let your car run 50,000 miles without an oil change, you shouldn't go months without updating your passwords or backing up your files.

The foundation of good cyber hygiene starts with **updates**. Make it a habit to check for updates on your devices, browsers, apps, and software tools. These updates often include critical security patches. Enable automatic updates whenever possible, and set a recurring calendar reminder to manually check your most important systems—like your website plugins, antivirus software, password manager, and operating system—at least once a week.

Next, focus on **password and account hygiene**. Use your password manager daily, not just for logging in, but for reviewing stored passwords. Remove logins you no longer use. Update any passwords that are duplicates, weak, or have been flagged as compromised. If your password manager offers security alerts, check them regularly and act immediately. Set a reminder to rotate your most sensitive passwords—like email, banking, and cloud storage—every 60 to 90 days.

Two-factor authentication (2FA) should be treated as non-negotiable. Every time you open a new account or app, make it a reflex to enable 2FA. Yes, it adds an extra step—but that step could block a hacker even if they've stolen your password. Review your 2FA settings periodically to ensure they're linked to an authenticator app rather than SMS, and that you have backup codes saved securely.

Backups are your safety net. A ransomware attack, stolen laptop, or corrupted file shouldn't erase years of work. Establish a backup routine that includes:

- **Daily automatic cloud backups** of active documents and apps.

- **Weekly local backups** to an encrypted external hard drive.
- **Monthly full-system snapshots** of your website, content, and media library.

Once you've set up your backups, **test them**. A backup that doesn't work when you need it is worse than no backup at all.

Your **email inbox** also needs regular cleaning. Archive old conversations. Delete emails with outdated links or sensitive information. Clear out spam and phishing attempts. Don't leave old receipts, login credentials, or client files sitting in your inbox indefinitely. Set up filters and folders so that only important messages land in your main view, reducing your chances of missing or mishandling a critical security alert.

Let's talk about **device behavior**. Start by locking your screen whenever you step away—even for a moment. Never leave your laptop open in a public place. If you work remotely or travel often, invest in a **privacy screen** to prevent visual hacking (when someone looks over your shoulder). Always **log out** of shared or public devices, and avoid storing passwords in browsers on computers you don't own.

Be cautious with **Wi-Fi usage**. Avoid logging into sensitive accounts when connected to public networks (airports, coffee shops, hotels). If you must use public Wi-Fi, always connect through a trusted **VPN (Virtual Private Network)**. VPNs encrypt your internet traffic, making it harder for anyone on the same network to spy on your activity.

Practice **digital minimalism**. Delete unused apps and browser extensions regularly. Every app you install is another potential access point for hackers. If you haven't used it in a month, remove it. This goes for mobile apps, desktop software, cloud tools, and browser add-ons. Less clutter means fewer vulnerabilities.

Create a simple **cyber hygiene calendar**. Here's a basic weekly structure:

- **Monday**: Check for software and app updates.
- **Wednesday**: Review password manager and 2FA alerts.
- **Friday**: Run a quick malware scan and verify backups.
- **End of month**: Audit access permissions on shared drives, remove unused logins, and delete unneeded files.

You can tailor this schedule to your business needs, but the goal is to make cybersecurity a routine—not a reaction.

Finally, build your **awareness muscle**. Subscribe to one or two trusted cybersecurity newsletters or podcasts—like *CyberScoop, Krebs on Security*, or *The Hacker News*. You don't need to become an expert, but staying aware of the latest scams, phishing tactics, and platform vulnerabilities can help you recognize warning signs early.

Here's your Cyber Hygiene Checklist:

1. **Enable automatic updates.** Set reminders to manually check priority systems weekly.

2. **Use and maintain a password manager.** Rotate sensitive passwords every 60–90 days.

3. **Activate and monitor 2FA.** Prefer app-based methods and save backup codes.

4. **Back up your files regularly.** Use cloud and local solutions—and test them.

5. **Clean your inbox.** Archive, delete, and set filters to control clutter.

6. **Log out of devices.** Use screen locks and avoid storing passwords in browsers.

7. **Use a VPN on public Wi-Fi.** Never log into sensitive accounts on unprotected networks.

8. **Delete unused apps and tools.** Reduce your attack surface by staying lean.

9. **Schedule cyber hygiene routines.** Make security a consistent part of your workflow.

10. **Stay informed.** Read or listen to one security update source each week.

Cyber hygiene isn't flashy. You won't get applause for locking your screen or updating your plugins. But these small daily actions are what stand between your thriving business and a devastating breach. Just like healthy eating or exercise, the results compound over time—and they're worth it.

The story of how Trevor started a morning security checklist

Trevor ran a successful online business designing e-book covers and promotional graphics for self-published authors. He'd built his client base through word of mouth and referrals, and his workflow was smooth: client fills out a form, Trevor designs the cover, they collaborate over email, and the final files are delivered through Google Drive. He had no employees, no physical office, and no fancy infrastructure. Just a laptop, a few design apps, and a loyal roster of returning clients.

That's why he was shocked when, one morning, his design files wouldn't open.

His computer screen displayed an unfamiliar message: *"Your files have been encrypted. Pay $500 in Bitcoin to recover your data."*

Trevor stared at the screen in disbelief. His laptop—his business, really—had been hit with ransomware. The worst part? He had no recent backups. The only copy of several active projects was locked on his hard drive, inaccessible unless he paid the attacker. And even then, there was no guarantee the files would be restored. One client was waiting for a cover due that day. Another had a book launch next week.

Trevor didn't know how the ransomware had gotten in. Maybe it was the file he downloaded last week, or maybe a browser extension he'd installed to speed up email templates. He had skipped system updates for months because they always interrupted his design sessions. His antivirus license had expired six weeks earlier, and he never renewed it. Passwords? Most were still stored in a plain text document on his desktop. He had always told himself he'd "deal with all that security stuff later."

Later never came.

In desperation, Trevor paid the ransom. A day later, he received a decryption key, but many of the files were still corrupted. He had to inform his clients. Some were understanding. Others weren't. One demanded a refund and left a bad review on his Fiverr profile. Another client simply disappeared and never replied again.

Once the smoke cleared, Trevor made a decision. He might not be able to undo the past, but he could change how he worked going forward. The next morning, he bought a new laptop. Before installing any design software, he set up a password manager and generated strong, unique passwords for all his accounts. He activated two-factor authentication everywhere—email, design tools, payment platforms.

He signed up for cloud backup software that ran automatically in the background and bought an external hard drive for weekly backups. Every Friday at 3 PM, a reminder popped up: *Run security scan. Backup files. Check 2FA settings.* It became part of his workday rhythm, like sending invoices or checking email.

He even created a "morning security checklist" that he reviewed each day before working:

- VPN connected?

- Password manager logged in?
- Files backed up from yesterday?
- No suspicious emails?

Little by little, Trevor rebuilt not just his systems, but his mindset. He realized cybersecurity wasn't about paranoia—it was about respect. Respect for his own time, for his clients' trust, and for the business he'd worked so hard to build.

He started cleaning his inbox weekly, deleting old attachments and clearing spam. He removed unused browser extensions, deleted apps that hadn't been opened in months, and unsubscribed from shady email lists. His computer ran faster, his mind felt clearer, and his clients noticed the difference. "You're more organized than ever," one commented.

He even shared what he'd learned with other freelancers in his network. He posted a thread on Twitter titled "How I Almost Lost My Business in 10 Seconds," outlining his story and the daily practices he'd adopted. The post went viral in his niche, and dozens of fellow creatives messaged him saying they'd started backing up their files and securing their accounts because of him.

Today, Trevor treats cybersecurity the same way he treats client deadlines: as a non-negotiable. He doesn't wait for things to break to fix them. He doesn't assume he's too small to be a target. And he doesn’t let convenience get in the way of protection.

Because he knows now that cyber hygiene isn’t optional. It’s how you stay in business.

Chapter 8: Crisis Mode — What to Do If You Get Hacked

Even with the best prevention, cyberattacks can still happen. Devices get stolen, passwords get leaked, and human error can leave a door open. When it does, your response in the next 60 minutes can determine whether you suffer a minor disruption—or a full-blown business disaster. This chapter will show you exactly what to do *step by step* if your accounts are compromised, your website is defaced, your data is encrypted, or your client information is exposed.

Let's start with the mindset: **Don't panic—act fast and systematically.** A clear plan allows you to minimize damage, regain control, and begin rebuilding trust with your clients and audience. Here's a crisis response framework that every entrepreneur and freelancer should have ready.

Step 1: Identify the Breach

Start by gathering clues:

- Were you locked out of an account?
- Is your website down or redirecting visitors?
- Did you notice unauthorized transactions or messages

sent from your email?

- Did your antivirus software flag a file or program?

The sooner you recognize something's wrong, the faster you can stop it from spreading. Check all your devices, accounts, and platforms for signs of tampering. Don't dismiss small red flags—random logouts, password resets you didn't request, or unfamiliar login notifications could be signs of a larger breach.

Step 2: Disconnect and Contain

If you suspect malware or a ransomware attack:

- **Disconnect from the internet** immediately.
- **Power off or isolate** affected devices.
- **Remove USBs, external drives, and backups** to prevent them from getting infected.

If it's an account-based breach (e.g., email or cloud platform):

- Log in (if possible) and change your password immediately.
- **Log out of all sessions** on all devices.
- **Revoke third-party app permissions** and integrations you don't recognize.

Don't attempt to fix things while still connected—contain the threat first.

Step 3: Change All Related Passwords

Assume that any login tied to the compromised system may be at risk. Use your password manager to:

- Change passwords on all high-value accounts (email, bank, cloud storage, social platforms).
- Generate strong, unique replacements.
- Enable 2FA where it wasn't previously set.

Be thorough—hackers often pivot from one account to others (called *lateral movement*), using credentials or access to reach connected platforms.

Step 4: Scan Devices and Recover Backups

Run a deep scan with antivirus and anti-malware tools on all devices involved. Use reputable tools like Malwarebytes, Bitdefender, or Windows Defender to detect and quarantine threats.

Once cleaned:

- Restore clean versions of files from **offline or cloud**

backups.

- Do *not* restore files from systems that may have been compromised.
- If your website was infected, work with your host or use services like Sucuri or Wordfence to scan, clean, and patch vulnerabilities.

Do not resume business operations until systems are verified safe.

Step 5: Notify Affected Clients and Partners

If client information was exposed, you must be transparent. Send a clear, professional message:

- Acknowledge the incident.
- Explain what data was affected (if known).
- Describe what you've done to contain the situation.
- Offer to answer questions and provide ongoing updates.

You don't need to disclose every technical detail—but honesty and speed are essential. Even if the breach didn't directly involve their data, your clients deserve to know what happened and how you're protecting them moving forward.

Step 6: Document the Incident

Create a log of everything:

- What happened and when.
- What you did to contain the threat.
- What accounts or systems were affected.
- What recovery steps were taken.

This will help you refine your security plan and may be required for legal, insurance, or platform reporting purposes (e.g., if your site violated a payment processor's terms or privacy laws).

Step 7: Report the Breach

Depending on the severity and nature of the breach:

- Report it to your website host, payment processor, or relevant platform.
- Notify your domain registrar if your DNS was hijacked.
- File a report with the **FTC (U.S.)** or local data protection authorities (e.g., GDPR regulators in Europe).

- If stolen funds or identity theft occurred, file a police report or notify your bank.

This paperwork matters for insurance claims, fraud protection, and in some cases, legal compliance.

Step 8: Learn, Fortify, and Rebuild Trust

Once the immediate crisis has passed, perform a **post-mortem**. What led to the breach? Was it a weak password? A missed update? A phishing email?

Then take action:

- Update your cyber hygiene routine.
- Implement stronger authentication and monitoring tools.
- Re-audit team access and client permissions.
- Create a formal incident response plan for future situations.

Finally, communicate openly with clients, subscribers, or users. Let them know what changed, how their data is safer now, and why you've taken security seriously since the breach.

Emergency Toolkit: Tools to Keep Ready

- Password manager with emergency access
- Antivirus and malware scanner
- Encrypted backup system (cloud + local)
- 2FA app with backup codes stored safely
- Template for client notification
- Access logs or audit trails (from cloud platforms)
- Contact info for your hosting support and domain registrar

Here's a quick checklist to follow in a breach:

1. **Detect**: Monitor signs of intrusion.
2. **Disconnect**: Isolate the threat.
3. **Change passwords**: Lock out unauthorized users.
4. **Scan & clean**: Remove malware.
5. **Restore**: Use clean backups.
6. **Notify**: Contact clients or partners transparently.
7. **Report**: File with relevant platforms or authorities.

8. **Review & improve**: Prevent the next attack.

Getting hacked is a nightmare—but it doesn't have to be the end of your business. A clear, confident response builds credibility, resilience, and a safer future.

What Nina did when she got hacked.

Nina had just wrapped up a record-breaking month for her online consulting business. Her email list had grown by 2,000 subscribers, her newest digital course was bringing in consistent passive income, and clients were leaving glowing testimonials on her site. On a quiet Sunday afternoon, she opened her laptop to respond to a few messages. But instead of her usual dashboard, she was greeted by a flashing red screen and a message she had only heard about in tech horror stories:

"Your data has been encrypted. Pay $1,200 in Bitcoin to regain access. You have 72 hours."

Nina froze.

She tried restarting her computer—same message. She plugged in her external hard drive to access a backup—nothing. The ransomware had spread there, too. Her heart pounded as she realized she had no cloud backup, no security plan, and no idea where to even begin. Her client files, video recordings, email sequences, invoices, contracts—all locked.

She panicked and called a tech-savvy friend. "Whatever you do," he warned, "don't pay the ransom. There's no guarantee you'll get your files back." Instead, he helped her take the first critical step: disconnecting from the internet. That stopped the malware from communicating with its controller and potentially infecting more files. Then they powered off her computer and began planning the recovery.

Over the next 48 hours, Nina learned more about cybersecurity than she had in the past five years combined. Her friend walked her through every step: booting the device in safe mode, using malware tools to assess the damage, scanning with multiple antivirus programs, and identifying the ransomware variant. Fortunately, one of the tools they used had a decryption key available. They recovered about 80% of her files. The rest were lost for good.

That week was a blur of emotions—relief, embarrassment, guilt, and determination. Nina spent hours contacting affected clients to let them know what happened. She explained the situation honestly, shared the steps she was taking to secure their data moving forward, and offered make-goods to anyone whose files had been affected. Most were sympathetic. One even said, "I appreciate your transparency. This could've happened to any of us."

But deep down, Nina knew it shouldn't have happened at all.

In the days that followed, she rebuilt her systems. She created a fresh digital workspace, wiped her infected drives, and installed commercial-grade antivirus software. She moved all active files to encrypted cloud storage and began daily cloud and weekly local backups. She adopted a password manager, enabled 2FA on every platform, and began using a secure VPN when working on public Wi-Fi.

More importantly, she documented the entire experience. She created a detailed "Crisis Recovery Plan" in Google Docs outlining what to do, who to call, and how to respond if anything like this ever happened again. She included template emails to send clients, a log of services to contact, and even drafted a checklist for the first 60 minutes of a breach.

As painful as the hack had been, it changed her forever. She realized that in a digital business, your *first job* is protecting the ecosystem you operate in. Every login, every file, every transaction deserves the same care you'd give your personal finances or physical workspace. "I was running a six-figure business on systems held together with hope," she admitted later. "Never again."

Her new approach became part of her brand. In one of her weekly emails to her list, she wrote about the hack in detail—how it happened, what she did to fix it, and what she learned. It was one of her most replied-to emails ever. People thanked her for being real. Others admitted they had zero backups or had never changed their passwords. Some even hired her to audit their own systems.

Now, Nina opens every new client engagement with a security check. She makes sure contracts are signed securely, file-sharing platforms are locked down, and sensitive data is exchanged only through encrypted channels. She encourages her clients to protect themselves too—not out of fear, but out of respect for their work.

Her business is safer. Her clients feel safer. And so does she.

The truth is, getting hacked isn't always the result of negligence. Sometimes it's bad luck. But recovery requires clarity, action, and honesty. Nina's story proves that how you respond is just as important as how you prepare.

She didn't just get her files back—she got her confidence back. And now, she helps others do the same.

Chapter 9: Tools & Resources for Ongoing Protection

Cybersecurity isn't just about reacting to problems—it's about building systems that make protection automatic and sustainable. As a busy entrepreneur or freelancer, you don't have time to constantly monitor every threat or read every tech bulletin. What you need is a reliable cybersecurity **toolkit**—a curated set of software, services, and strategies that protect your business while you work.

This chapter introduces essential tools and resources to keep your digital operations safe. Think of it as your security command center—ready to scale with your business and adapt as threats evolve.

Password Managers

At the core of every secure system is strong password management. Using unique, complex passwords for every account is no longer optional—and storing them in your head or browser is a risk. Instead, use a **password manager** to generate, store, and auto-fill secure passwords.

Recommended Tools:

- **1Password** – Great for individuals and small teams; intuitive interface.
- **Bitwarden** – Open-source, highly secure, and has a generous free plan.
- **Dashlane** – Offers password health reports and dark web monitoring.

Look for features like 2FA integration, encrypted storage, password sharing, and cross-device syncing. Set reminders to update key passwords regularly.

Two-Factor Authentication (2FA) Apps

Even the best password can be compromised. Two-factor authentication adds a second layer of protection by requiring a time-sensitive code generated from a separate device.

Recommended Apps:

- **Authy** – Offers encrypted backups and multi-device support.
- **Google Authenticator** – Simple and widely supported.
- **Microsoft Authenticator** – Great for Microsoft ecosystem users.

Avoid SMS-based 2FA when possible. It's vulnerable to SIM-swapping attacks. Use app-based 2FA instead.

Antivirus & Anti-Malware Protection

Whether you're using Mac, Windows, or Linux, you need strong malware protection. These tools detect threats, block infected downloads, and scan files and devices in real-time.

Recommended Tools:

- **Malwarebytes** – Easy to use, excellent at detecting spyware and ransomware.
- **Bitdefender** – Lightweight and highly rated across all devices.
- **Windows Defender** – Built into Windows 10/11 and effective when paired with good hygiene.

Keep real-time scanning enabled and run weekly system scans. Set up email alerts for detections.

Secure Cloud Storage

Store and back up sensitive files in encrypted, cloud-based systems that support permission-based sharing, version history, and zero-knowledge encryption.

Recommended Services:

- **Google Workspace** – Business-grade controls, file history, access management.
- **Proton Drive** – End-to-end encrypted cloud storage.
- **Dropbox Business** – Audit trails, file locking, and secure team collaboration.

Organize files by sensitivity, use encrypted folders for private data, and revoke sharing links regularly.

Virtual Private Networks (VPNs)

VPNs encrypt your internet connection, protecting your activity on public Wi-Fi and hiding your IP address. They're essential if you travel, work remotely, or often connect outside your home or office.

Recommended VPNs:

- **NordVPN** – Fast, secure, and beginner-friendly.
- **ExpressVPN** – Strong privacy record and works well internationally.
- **ProtonVPN** – Free plan available; based in privacy-friendly Switzerland.

Avoid free, ad-supported VPNs—they often sell your data or lack encryption.

Backup Systems

You should always have at least two backups: one in the cloud and one local.

Recommended Solutions:

- **Backblaze** – Continuous cloud backup, affordable pricing.
- **iDrive** – Combines file syncing, cloud backup, and disk imaging.
- **Time Machine (Mac) / File History (Windows)** – Local backup systems that restore full device states.

Test your backups every month to ensure they're actually working and restorable.

Website Security Tools

If you run a website or e-commerce store, use security plugins, monitoring tools, and firewall services.

Recommended Tools:

- **Wordfence** (WordPress) – Firewall, malware

scanning, login protection.

- **Sucuri** – Site monitoring, cleanup, CDN, and advanced protection.
- **Cloudflare** – Free DDoS protection and performance optimization.

Install alerts for suspicious activity, limit login attempts, and scan for malware regularly.

Email & Phishing Protection

Your email is your digital identity. Protect it with strong spam filtering, suspicious login alerts, and secure access protocols.

Add-ons and Features to Enable:

- SPF, DKIM, and DMARC on your domain.
- Use **ProtonMail** or **Zoho Mail** for encrypted business email.
- Email scanning tools like Mimecast or Barracuda for larger teams.

Regularly review account login history and connected apps.

Threat Monitoring & Alerts

Keep track of your exposure using dark web scans and data breach monitoring tools.

Recommended Tools:

- **Have I Been Pwned** – Check if your email or password has been exposed.
- **DeHashed** – Advanced search tool for leaked credentials.
- **Firefox Monitor** – Automated alerts for breaches affecting your accounts.

Subscribe to these services for real-time alerts and respond quickly to any flagged credentials.

Ongoing Learning & News

Cybersecurity evolves fast. Staying informed ensures you're not caught off guard by new threats.

Recommended Sources:

- **The Hacker News**
- **CyberScoop**
- **Krebs on Security**

- **Smashing Security Podcast**
- **Google Alerts** for terms like "freelancer breach" or "cloud security"

Set aside 15 minutes per week to skim relevant articles or listen to one podcast episode.

Final Tips for Sustainable Protection

- **Keep your tools simple and consistent.** Choose one password manager, one antivirus, and one backup method and stick to them.
- **Automate whenever possible.** Scheduled scans, auto-backups, and update reminders reduce human error.
- **Review quarterly.** Set a recurring date every 3 months to audit your systems, permissions, and software.

You don't need a massive cybersecurity budget to stay safe. With the right tools and a few smart routines, you can protect your online business from 95% of the most common threats—and get back to doing what you do best.

Jordan's freelancer story

Jordan was a freelance UX designer who prided himself on efficiency. He ran his business from a single laptop, used a handful of design apps, and stored everything in a beautifully organized Google Drive. Clients loved his clean deliverables and smooth process. But beneath the polished surface, Jordan had a blind spot: he had no real cybersecurity system.

For years, he'd relied on memory and luck. His passwords were saved in Chrome, most didn't have two-factor authentication, and his only "backup" was a Dropbox folder synced to his laptop. He told himself he didn't need extra tools—he wasn't a tech company, and he hadn't had any problems.

Until one day, he did.

It started small. A new design client emailed him asking, "Hey, did you just request my login info via a Google Form?" Confused, Jordan checked his inbox. Nothing. But then another client asked the same thing. And another. Panic set in. He checked his sent mail and realized someone had accessed his email account, created a fake form asking for credentials, and sent it out to every recent contact.

It was a scam—and it had come from *his* account.

The attacker had likely used a leaked password from one of Jordan's old accounts. Since he reused passwords across platforms, they were able to break into his Gmail, create a malicious Google Form, and send it to clients using his real name and address. In the eyes of his clients, it looked like Jordan was the scammer.

He spent the next 24 hours cleaning up the mess. He changed his passwords, enabled 2FA, emailed everyone he could think of with an apology and warning, and deleted the form. Most of his clients were forgiving. But one new client walked away. They didn't feel safe.

That was the wake-up call Jordan needed.

He spent the rest of the week researching cybersecurity tools. First, he ditched Chrome's built-in password storage and downloaded Bitwarden. Within an hour, he had created strong, unique passwords for all his accounts and stored them safely. He installed Authy on his phone and enabled two-factor authentication on Gmail, Stripe, Trello, and every other platform he used.

He replaced his outdated antivirus software with Malwarebytes and set it to scan daily. Then he discovered that his Dropbox files weren't really backed up—they were mirrored. If something was deleted or corrupted on his device, it would reflect in the cloud. He signed up for Backblaze and started automatic backups of his entire system, including versioned archives.

Jordan also realized he'd been using a ton of browser extensions without even thinking. Some were outdated. A few were from unknown developers. He removed everything except what he used weekly. He installed a VPN and made it a habit to activate it whenever he worked outside his home office. He even added a privacy screen to his laptop—something he never thought he needed until he caught a stranger glancing at his screen in a café.

Over time, these tools became second nature. He created a monthly security routine: update software, rotate a few key passwords, check login histories, and verify his backups were working. He no longer relied on hope—he had a system.

He also documented his setup. He created a private Notion page listing his cybersecurity tools, backup schedule, 2FA recovery codes, and links to each service. If anything happened to his device or he needed to onboard a team member in the future, he was ready.

To his surprise, clients started noticing. One complimented the secure file-sharing links he now used. Another appreciated that his contracts were digitally signed and encrypted. One even said, "You're the first freelancer I've worked with who seems to care about digital safety. It makes a difference."

Jordan didn't stop there. He began mentoring other designers, teaching them how to build a basic cybersecurity toolkit. "You don't have to be a tech genius," he told them. "You just have to respect your clients, your data, and your time."

The breach had been painful—but it became the catalyst for real growth. Jordan now ran a lean, secure business. He didn't feel anxious when opening his inbox. He knew he had the right tools in place. More importantly, he felt professional in a new way—not just in his designs, but in how he operated behind the scenes.

Because in today's digital world, it's not just what you deliver that matters—it's how you protect the trust that comes with it.

Chapter 10: Cybersecurity as a Business Advantage

In most industries, cybersecurity is viewed as a defensive measure—something you do to protect yourself from loss. But in the world of freelancing, consulting, and digital entrepreneurship, cybersecurity can actually become a **competitive advantage**. Clients aren't just hiring you for your talent—they're trusting you with sensitive information, business strategies, intellectual property, and in some cases, access to their systems. Demonstrating that you take cybersecurity seriously can set you apart from competitors, build long-term trust, and open doors to higher-quality contracts.

Let's start with the **psychology of trust**. When a client decides to work with you, they're doing more than purchasing a service—they're extending a relationship. That relationship is built on the assumption that their data, identity, and communication are safe with you. Every time you send a document, ask for login credentials, or share a link, you're either reinforcing or eroding that trust.

By practicing visible cybersecurity—such as using password-protected links, encrypted contracts, and secure messaging—you send a signal: "I care about your information as much as I care about mine." This is particularly powerful in industries where data privacy matters deeply, like coaching, consulting, digital marketing, law, real estate, finance, and healthcare.

Clients notice the little things. When you share files using Google Drive with specific permissions instead of "Anyone with the link," or use platforms like DocuSign or PandaDoc with access controls, it shows a level of professionalism that others skip. Even small actions—like asking clients not to send passwords over email or proactively explaining how you'll store their data—position you as someone who takes their role seriously.

Freelancers and business owners who lead with security often earn better referrals and repeat business. Why? Because people want to feel safe. They want to know that their hard work won't be leaked, stolen, or lost due to a freelancer's oversight. This is especially true when working with clients in corporate settings or regulated industries. Increasingly, companies are adding digital security questions to contractor onboarding forms. Being able to say, "Yes, I use 2FA and encrypted backups," can mean the difference between landing or losing a project.

Cybersecurity can also be a powerful **sales and positioning tool**. When writing proposals or onboarding new clients, include a "Data Protection & Privacy" section. Briefly outline your security measures: how you store files, how you manage passwords, and what protocols are in place in case of a breach. You don't need to write a technical manual—just a short paragraph that demonstrates awareness and preparedness.

Example:

> "All client information is stored securely using encrypted cloud storage with role-based access. Passwords are managed through a secure password vault, and two-factor authentication is enabled across all project tools. File access is time-limited and revoked upon project completion."

You can also include a link to a short "Digital Security Statement" on your website or in your proposal documents. This small touch goes a long way in establishing credibility and can help justify premium pricing. After all, clients aren't just paying for what you do—they're paying for peace of mind.

Next, let's talk about **compliance readiness**. Even if you're not legally required to follow regulations like GDPR, HIPAA, or CCPA, aligning your business practices with their principles demonstrates leadership. It shows that you think like a pro. For example:

- Using tools that are GDPR-compliant.
- Storing only the data you need.
- Having a data deletion policy.
- Informing clients how their information will be used.

All of these add to your trust profile.

In group coaching programs, online courses, or membership communities, security can also be a **retention strategy**. People want to stay in environments that feel well-managed and safe. By securing member areas, moderating file-sharing, and implementing login protections, you build a space that feels intentional and high-value.

Public perception matters too. With cybercrime constantly in the news, people are more security-conscious than ever. If they see that your business is organized, protected, and transparent about its processes, they'll be more likely to trust you with bigger opportunities.

Here are some ways to turn cybersecurity into a business advantage:

1. **Include a Security Section in Proposals** Briefly outline your protection practices.

2. **Brand Your Safety Practices** Create a branded "Client Trust Policy" or "Privacy Promise."

3. **Add Credentials to Your Website** Display logos of tools you use (e.g., LastPass, Sucuri, ProtonMail).

4. **Use Branded, Secure File Sharing** Share files from your domain or branded folders with access logs.

5. **Discuss Security During Onboarding** Frame it as a value add: "Here's how I keep your data safe."

6. **Include it in Testimonials or Case Studies** Ask clients to mention how safe or secure your process felt.

7. **Offer Security Reviews as a Bonus** For clients with weak systems, offer to audit their process as part of your service.

8. **Charge More for Being Reliable** Position your professionalism (including security) as a reason you're worth premium rates.

Security isn't boring—it's branding. In a marketplace crowded with freelancers and small businesses, professionalism, reliability, and trust are your greatest assets. Cybersecurity, when done well and communicated clearly, reinforces all three.

Shayla's story

Shayla was a brand consultant who worked with luxury wellness companies and premium service providers. Her work went beyond logos and fonts—she helped her clients craft messaging, launch products, and position themselves at the high end of their market. Most of her clients came through referrals, and nearly all were sensitive about discretion. Many of them were launching businesses quietly, preparing major rebrands, or protecting intellectual property before it hit the market.

Shayla understood image. She understood premium service. But for a long time, she didn't understand just how much cybersecurity could reinforce her brand.

That changed during a client discovery call.

Her new client, an executive coach building a private membership platform for C-suite women, asked a question Shayla hadn't expected: "How do you store the strategy docs and launch plans we'll be working on? Are those files encrypted?"

Shayla paused.

She had never been asked that before. She usually used Google Drive with open links, shared PDFs via email, and stored her notes in Notion. She used two-factor authentication but had never thought to formalize her file storage or create a data policy.

"I'll walk you through my process," Shayla replied smoothly—then spent the next hour that night rebuilding it from scratch.

She realized that her clients weren't just investing in design—they were trusting her with plans worth tens or hundreds of thousands of dollars. Product names, copywriting drafts, investor decks, pricing structures—all of it sat inside her unstructured folders with generic permissions. And if one email were hacked or one link leaked, that trust would be gone.

Over the next week, she transformed her entire backend system. She adopted Proton Drive for encrypted file storage and shared only with email-specific access and expiration dates. She used PandaDoc for contracts, added password protection to all brand guides and strategy decks, and created a formal "Client Privacy & Data Protection" policy that she included in every onboarding package.

But Shayla didn't stop at tightening her systems—she began showcasing them.

On her website, she added a section titled: **"Your Trust is Protected Here."** It explained, in simple language, how she safeguarded client data. During onboarding, she walked clients through her security practices. Instead of saying, "I'll email you the link," she said, "I'll send you a private, encrypted download with 7-day access—no one but you will ever see this."

Her clients noticed. Some told her they'd never worked with a service provider who treated their data with such respect. One referred a colleague specifically because of how "professional and secure" Shayla felt. Another said, "This isn't just design—it's a luxury experience."

And that's when it clicked.

Security was no longer just something Shayla did in the background. It was part of her *branding*. It was part of what made her premium. While other freelancers competed on price or turnaround time, she competed on confidence. Clients trusted her not just to deliver—but to protect what mattered most.

She even created a downloadable PDF titled **"The Digital Trust Checklist"**—a gift she gave to every new client. It included basic security tips like using 2FA, how to spot phishing emails, and how to protect creative assets before launch. That little checklist became a powerful brand touchpoint—something her clients shared with their teams and referred back to often.

One client said, "You made me realize that branding and protection go hand in hand. I didn't know how much I needed this."

Over time, Shayla raised her rates. She didn't just promise deliverables—she promised discretion, security, and peace of mind. And she backed it up with tools, transparency, and systems that made clients feel like they were in expert hands.

Now, Shayla mentors other creative entrepreneurs on how to bring more professionalism into their process. She teaches them that cybersecurity isn't just a tech thing—it's a trust thing. That in an age of constant hacks and data leaks, being the *secure* option is being the *smart* option.

Her final lesson? "Your brand is everything the client *experiences*, even behind the scenes. If you can make them feel safe, they'll stick with you—because safety is rare, and rare is valuable."

Epilogue

Cybersecurity used to feel like something reserved for big corporations, tech startups, or the ultra-wealthy. It conjured up images of firewalls, complex code, and rooms filled with blinking servers. But today, in our hyperconnected world, cybersecurity is something **every entrepreneur and freelancer** must embrace—not just to prevent problems, but to elevate their professionalism, protect their reputation, and build real, lasting trust with clients.

This book wasn't written to scare you. It was written to *equip* you.

Because the truth is, the digital world we work in now demands more than talent or hustle. It demands **ownership**. And part of owning a business—whether you're running a solo operation or leading a small team—is owning the responsibility to protect what you build. Your projects, your files, your emails, your contracts, your brand assets, your client information—all of it deserves security. Not because something *might* happen, but because the cost of inaction is too high to ignore.

Throughout this book, we've walked through the real-world foundations of digital protection. You learned how to:

- Secure your devices and accounts.
- Protect sensitive client data.
- Detect phishing and email threats.
- Lock down your website and payment systems.
- Work with clients and contractors securely.
- Build daily cyber hygiene habits.
- Respond quickly and confidently in a crisis.
- Use practical tools to automate your defenses.
- Turn cybersecurity into a powerful *business advantage.*

What you've built, what you're building, and what you *will* build in the future—it's all worth safeguarding. And now, you know how.

But here's the final, most important point: **Cybersecurity is no longer optional—it's your new standard of professionalism.**

When you consistently demonstrate digital security, you're not just protecting yourself from fraud or inconvenience. You're signaling to the world that you're serious, capable, and worthy of trust. You stand out not only for your talent, but for your structure. You become the provider people return to and refer—not because you were the cheapest, but because they *felt safe* with you.

That's a rare quality in a noisy, insecure world. And rare is powerful.

If you've followed along and started implementing even half of what we covered, you're already ahead of most small businesses. Most people wait until something breaks to fix it. But not you. You've chosen the proactive path—the empowered path.

Still, cybersecurity isn't a destination. It's a rhythm. The good news? Once it's built into your routine, it becomes second nature. You don't have to live in fear. You just live smarter. Cleaner. Clearer. Stronger. You wake up each day knowing that your tools are working for you—even when you're not watching.

And that is the real gift: **peace of mind.**

You can focus on what you love—coaching, designing, writing, consulting, building, innovating—because your systems are sound. Your processes are professional. Your clients are protected. Your business is resilient. You've become the kind of entrepreneur who doesn't just *deliver* excellence—you **defend** it.

And that? That's worth everything.

Thank you for listening to Book 8 of the Cyber Shield Academy Series. Stay sharp. Stay safe. And above all, stay trusted.

Your future depends on it.

www.ingramcontent.com/pod-product-compliance
Lightning Source LLC
LaVergne TN
LVHW022006200926
848481LV00007B/2265
9798349645273